MW00475501

HOLY
HOT
MESS

guided journal

HOLY HOT MESS

guided journal

MARY KATHERINE BACKSTROM

WORTHY
PUBLISHING

New York • Nashville

Worthy
Hachette Book Group
1290 Avenue of the Americas, New York, NY 10104
worthypublishing.com
twitter.com/worthypub

First Edition: September 2023

Worthy is a division of Hachette Book Group, Inc. The Worthy name and logo are trademarks of Hachette Book Group, Inc.

The publisher is not responsible for websites (or their content) that are not owned by the publisher.

The Hachette Speakers Bureau provides a wide range of authors for speaking events. To find out more, go to hachettespeakersbureau.com or email HachetteSpeakers@hbgusa.com.

Worthy Books may be purchased in bulk for business, educational, or promotional use. For information, please contact your local bookseller or the Hachette Book Group Special Markets Department at special.markets@hbgusa.com.

Print book interior design by Bart Dawson.

ISBN: 978-1-5460-1367-9

Printed in Canada

FRI

10 9 8 7 6 5 4 3 2 1

CONTENTS

Preface vii

CHAPTER 1
Check Under the Car Seat 1

CHAPTER 2
Ursus Arctos Horribilis 8

CHAPTER 3
A Tale of Two T—Um, I Mean, Cities. 16

CHAPTER 4
Sand and Water 23

CHAPTER 5
Ghosts and Guinea Pigs 30

CHAPTER 6
Welcome to Church, Everyone's Weird Here. 37

CHAPTER 7
On Sharks and Therapists 45

CHAPTER 8
Two Truths and a Lie 52

CHAPTER 9
Find Your Fellow Goat Thieves 58

CONTENTS

CHAPTER 10

Anniversary Rats. 65

CHAPTER 11

Baggage Claim. 72

CHAPTER 12

Birth Is a Messy Affair 78

CHAPTER 13

The Magic of the Moon 85

CHAPTER 14

Guardrails and Pool Noodles 93

CHAPTER 15

Life on the Hamster Wheel 100

CHAPTER 16

The Messiness Was the Point. 108

Scripture Credits. 115

PREFACE

There was a time that to talk about a *mess* meant a meal. It was about gathering and sharing a "mess," food that was sustaining and company that was community. It's why your cafeteria at summer church camp was called the *mess hall*. It's why the military still refers to meals on base or in the field as mess. There was even the great word *messmate* used at the time, to refer to someone you ate mess with, your pal at the dinner table.

Messmate. We've gotta bring that back.

But language is a dynamic and ever-changing phenomenon. And so, through the years, *mess* came to mean not just meals, but also when things are untidy, chaotic, and dirty. Which is ironic, because some etymologists (which is a fancy-pants word for people who study the development of words) think that the word *mess* came to mean what it does today because of a mispronunciation or misspelling of the word *muss. Muss* actually does mean something that is untidy and did long before *mess* showed up as the shiny new kid at vocabulary school.

So, yes, how we even got the word *mess* is a mess.

Seems fitting, right?

MK Backstrom has been a student of mess all her life, a hilarious and poignant storyteller about all the ways mess is evident in our lives and the ways God works with our mess to make us holy. And this journal, based on her best-selling book *Holy Hot Mess*, will take you on the journey of recognizing the messes in your life, both the ones that are obvious and maybe the ones you haven't realized before, and will show you God's purpose in it all.

This journal is designed for you to use alongside the book, a way to capture the insights and aha moments you'll experience along the way. So, if you don't already have it, be sure to get a copy of *Holy Hot Mess* to use along with the journal.

In the journal you'll find a short devotional reading that corresponds to each of the chapters in the book. After you complete each devotional reading, you'll find a series of journaling prompts. And each reading and journaling session ends with a guided prayer concerning the topic on which you've been reading and writing.

Check this out: You can't *mess* up in the way you use this journal. Only have time to answer a question today and maybe one tomorrow while you're waiting in the school pickup line? Great! Wanting to reclaim some time in the morning for yourself and looking for a guided journal that will give you spiritual sustenance to last throughout your day? Fantastic! Maybe you want to answer the journal prompts with only a few words or maybe you like to compose paragraphs. Make the experience your own. Whether you're a journal-entry-a-day type or only have time for a flyby every now and then, your time spent in this journal will leave you encouraged and curious. Laughing and misty-eyed. More aware of and more okay with your mess than ever. And you'll discover God is waiting there for you, in all the wild and unplanned and topsy-turvy days of your life.

You never have to feel alone in your mess, as if you're the only person who struggles and questions. You'll discover that you've got a friend in MK, someone who has lived out all kinds of messy adventures and who keeps looking and finding God in it all.

A messmate. That's what you'll find in these pages. A messmate along for the ride as you record your own Holy Hot Mess and see the wonder of God in what you write.

Now go make a gorgeous mess.

CHAPTER 1

CHECK UNDER THE CAR SEAT

We are living in a time that doesn't have much patience with mess. We like home renovations to show us quick-turnaround before and afters, all within the confines of a thirty-minute show. We give all the hearts to social media posts that serve up a two-frame picture of the pre– and post–weight loss and fitness journey. We drool over the pantry-organizing TikTok that sweeps across cluttered shelves and spins out color-coordinated snacks in matching clear bins, all set to a lo-fi rendition of an Abba song.

If there's going to be a mess, we want it rectified and swept up as quickly as possible.

But what if the truth of mortal life on this planet is that we can never outrun, outrenovate, outclean, or outorganize the mess? The mess inside our own emotions. The mess that shows up in our relationships. The mess in the junk drawers of our kitchens and our hearts.

In *Holy Hot Mess*, MK Backstrom asks you to consider that the goal is not to banish the mess in your life but to recognize that mess is simply part of being a God-created and God-loved human.

Our world often sells us the lie that we can somehow clean and scrub everything about ourselves to perfection. But the world isn't the only one fibbing to us. We lie to ourselves about this situation. We think we can stuff all the ratty, ugly, mismatched things about ourselves down a cosmic commode and flush it all away. But universal plumbing has a way of bringing things back up to the surface. And when a lie about our mess comes bubbling up to the surface and spills onto the scrubbed floors, it makes the mess even messier.

MK tried it. In an attempt to win the love of the coolest boy in gymnastics class, she ditched her old nasty socks and shoplifted herself a fresh pair from the gym's store. A clandestine re-socking in the ladies' room, a toss of the sales tags and old socks into the toilet, a flush of the bowl, and MK thought she had gotten away with her sock heist scot-free. But the gym pipes refused to be complicit in her crime and spit back up all the evidence. And then some.

She says, "Truth can be an uncomfortable friend. Life is hard, and sometimes owning our imperfect reality can feel like a stab in the heart. But at least when truth hurts, the injury is clean and quick. On the flip side, lies are made of jagged edges. The wounds they cause are messy and not so easily healed."

Not all the ways we try to cover who we are come gurgling up so quickly. Sometimes, we put a lot of effort and filter into hiding behind a manufactured image. MK calls this the Lie of Curation, when we continue to spin out the falsehood that we've got it all together. She says, "We are just showing up, putting the most beautiful versions of ourselves on display, and hoping to find real community and love. What's happening is quite the opposite. When we hide our messy, authentic selves from people, we are never truly seen. Instead, we invest so much time in this bizarre world that we buy into the lie that it is real."

It sounds counterintuitive to how we're taught to show up in the school pickup line, in the boardroom, and in the church pew, to express and embrace our mess instead of shushing it and sending it to the nearest corner. The Lie of Curation may sound like a new problem, one contingent on social media filters and highly edited content. But it's not. People have been up to this kind of stuff long before Instagram developed its ever-changing algorithms. Jesus said of the religious of His day, those who acted like being a mess wasn't a *thing* for them, "You are like white-washed tombs, which look beautiful on the outside but on the inside are full of the bones of the dead and everything unclean" (Matt. 23:27 NIV).

Could it be true that God would much rather we let our mess be seen than to hide it away? And what would change in your life if you lived that way?

For one, we might find that we have deeper connections with other people. When we tell the truth about who we are, we are letting ourselves be seen. Sure, there will be those who can't handle it. But that's not who you want to be deeply connected to anyway. Truth telling means there will be truth in your relationships. There will be truth in your faith community. And you'll likely know your people better as well, as they feel able to share their truths. As MK says, "There is something deeply connective about the fact that we are all just a little bit messy."

JOURNALING

Who is someone in your life that you desperately wanted to impress? What measures were you willing to go to?

....

....

....

....

Did you have a time in your life when you tried to hide a mistake you made? What happened?

....

....

....

....

How much of your life are you currently hiding away or only showing through a filter of verbiage?

....

....

....

....

On a scale of 1 to 10, how much do you think you struggle with trying to stuff parts of yourself away, with 1 being "Not at all" and 10 being "It feels like a constant state"?

1   2   3   4   5   6   7   8   9   10

When did that struggle start for you?

....

....

....

....

....

....

How do you typically try to hide your mess? Is it through trying to have the perfect house, eating and exercise habits that are exhausting, or shopping? What is it for you?

....

....

....

....

....

....

PRAYER

· · · · · · · · · · ·

God, it's tempting to make external perfection a primary goal in my life. I confess that I often worry more about presenting the right image than having the right heart. And I struggle to believe that You will accept me, and that there are people who will accept me, if I show just what a mess I am. Help me have the courage to be honest. Give me the wisdom to know who to be real with. For those places where I need extra help to unstuff, guide me to the right counselor or mentor who can help me in a healthy and healing way. Shine a light on those places that have gone dark for me, for the quirks I submerge, for the laughter I stifle, for the dreams I ignore. Let me live in the truth of who I am, not in the lie of who I think I have to be to receive love. In the name of Jesus, amen.

CHAPTER 2

URSUS ARCTOS HORRIBILIS

Somehow the concept of unconditional love has come to mean being embraced for all you are, with no restraints, no commentary, no guidance. But what if that's a slightly cheaper kind of love, a love that doesn't always have your best at heart?

Ursus arctos horribilis is the Latin for grizzly bear, and it seems no accident that the same species from which we proclaim Mama Bear is also the species with *horribilis* in its scientific name. A mother roaring in defense of her children can be an awesome, terrifying, powerful, and, yes, *horribilis* sight. And that image of a mama bear and her cubs isn't just our invention. God says it of Himself in Hosea 13, where He describes His response to enemies coming against His people: "Like a bear robbed of her cubs, I will attack them and rip them open" (v. 8 NIV).

But just like a mama bear will fight and protect and defend her cubs from danger and strangers, she'll probably also protect them from themselves when behaviors, choices, and habits that don't serve them well come into play.

There's a love that makes excuses, ignores danger, and avoids confrontation. Ironically, that kind of love can feel better, just like buttercream icing tastes better than broccoli. And because it feels better, that kind of love has somehow earned the rarefied moniker of *unconditional love*. MK writes about her mother's initial support of MK's backyard Olympic training, training that morphed from a goal of being on the gymnastics team to running hurdles over a broomstick, as one does. But when Momma sees MK about to attempt a late-session jump over a rusty gate with her opposite leg, Momma steps in. She levels with MK about the condition of the gate, the lateness of the evening, and MK's fatigue after running around the backyard on a loop. MK writes, "But what did Momma know about dreams? What did she know about glory?"

MK learns the answer in real time when she ends up in the ER with twenty-five stitches to her name. And she recounts other lessons she also had to learn in real time, things her mother had warned her about that she ignored, thinking Momma was trying to dampen her freedom and dreams. Ultimately MK discovers this:

> She wasn't trying to steal my sunshine. She wasn't trying to cramp my style. She wasn't some killjoy know-it-all who couldn't let me live for myself. She was a mother whose heart existed outside of her body. Who loved me ferociously and wanted to keep me from harm. Her hopes and plans for me were always for my good.

We sometimes want to make God fit into our notion of unconditional love. We want the part where He cheers us on and agrees with all of our plans. But as it turns out, God *is* love, meaning He gets to define what love is, how it operates, where it makes peace and where it fights, where it whispers, and where it roars. Sometimes God tells us it's a bad idea to jump over a rusty gate. Sometimes we don't want to hear it because it doesn't feel like our version of unconditional love. But as the very essence of what love is, it's God's way of being a mama bear that shows us what the fullest, most extravagant kind of love is all about. The writer of Hebrews says this:

> *My child, don't underestimate the value of the discipline and training of the Lord God, or get depressed when he*

has to correct you. For the Lord's training of your life is the evidence of his faithful love. And when he draws you to himself, it proves you are his delightful child. (12:5–6 TPT)

Here's the other side of the coin.

Sometimes, we go too far to the other side. We can think that love is available to us only if we act right, talk right, *are* right. Sometimes that's the only time we seemed to receive our parents' affection and attention in childhood, when we were performing up to par. Sometimes that's what we've been told from the pulpit, that we get God's love only when we measure up. But the mystery and reach of God's love, His version of unconditional, grace-based, sacrifice-paid, all-sufficient, eternal love, is something so much more.

MK gives us an incredible example of what that love can look like if we have the eyes to see it. She says of her mother:

She made the absolute most out of my absolute least. She celebrated the fact I existed. Of course, she wanted me to apply myself, to try harder as a student in school. I'm sure it kept her up at night. She is a mother, after all. But her pride in me, her motherly love, was never performance based. She wanted nothing more than for her daughter to be a "blue ribbon" student. But if that's not where I was, no matter the reason, she accepted me all the same. More than that, she fought for my joy. She celebrated every small win.

A mama bear kind of love, the kind God says He has for us? It's both. It's protective and ferocious, corrective and collective, honest and celebratory. No matter how messy we get, we have an Eternal Parent who sees our mess for what it is, guides us through it, and loves us no matter what. That's the best kind of unconditional love, the kind that sees our condition, loves us enough to guide us in truth, and celebrates us for who we are.

JOURNALING
· · · · · · · · · · · · · · · · · ·

How have you defined unconditional love in your life? Is there anything about that definition that might need to change?

· ·

· ·

· ·

· ·

If you are a parent, how has your view of love changed in loving your child?

· ·

· ·

· ·

· ·

What was something you attempted that those around you who were wiser and wanted only good for you tried to warn you about?

· ·

· ·

· ·

· ·

Write about something someone has done for you that is simply a celebration of who you are instead of rewarding you for what you've accomplished. Why do you think we're so much quicker as a culture to celebrate accomplishments or milestones instead of simply celebrating people?

....

....

....

....

....

....

Do you find it difficult to accept someone's love for you if it's not based on your performance? Why or why not?

....

....

....

....

....

....

....

....

PRAYER

· · · · · · · · · · ·

God, help me recognize when someone demonstrates exceptional love for me by sharing guidance and wisdom with me. Give me the knowledge and maturity to recognize the best kind of unconditional love instead of the world's vague definition of it. Help me forge stronger relationships with those who know how to celebrate me for who I am instead of how I perform. And Lord, let me be the same kind of friend and family for those You have brought into my life, loving my people for who they are instead of what they can do for me. In the name of Jesus, amen.

CHAPTER 3

A TALE OF TWO T—UM, I MEAN, CITIES

They're sisters, not twins.

At least, that's the assurance medical professionals give us.

We're talking boobs. Rarely do they match, neither each other nor our expectations. Those of us in the flat-chested camp may have always longed for a fluffier set. Those of us in the buxom camp may have wanted our girls to just settle down.

And MK?

Well, she started using prayer on hers. As in the get-these-things-outta-here kind of prayers. But the intent of her prayers versus where she ended up were two different things.

In chapter 3, MK hilariously and poignantly recounts the bad case of The Boobs she contracted in middle school. They kept her from playing sports she loved to play. They were a pain to find bras for, in a literal sense. She writes:

I just kept on growing. So being the sixth grader that I was, I came up with the brilliant solution of wearing four sports bras at a time, one on top of the other, until my chest was practically concave. I was pleased as punch with this idea and everything was working just fine.

That was, until the day Momma picked me up from school and informed me that we were going shopping. "It's time to get an appropriate bra," she said. "You look like a giant tube of sausage is sitting on your chest." I opened my mouth to protest, but she cut me off. "You can't just make curves *disappear*. When you smash them down, they have to go *somewhere*. It's science, sweetie."

"Well, I hate science," I responded.

And when MK gave birth to her first child, she discovered that she struggled mightily to breastfeed, a situation that seemed epically unfair, given that she was hauling around epically large breasts.

She found herself again praying for the things to fall off.

MK thought she'd found her miracle in a breast-reduction surgery that made her case of The Boobs manageable. But a routine tissue sample taken during that procedure revealed that she had breast cancer, and the breast reduction ultimately ended up in a second surgery, a mastectomy.

It seemed a cruel turn of events. MK confesses, "When your prayer for your boobs to go away becomes cancer, when your prayer for that job becomes a soul-draining situation, when your prayer for the right guy becomes a broken heart, it's hard to see God in any of it. And worse, if He's there, it kinda makes you wonder: Is He intentionally breaking my heart?"

The kind and powerful observation of her nurse helped MK change her perspective. If MK had not had an overflowing case of The Boobs, she might not have sought the reduction surgery. Without the reduction surgery, because of how unusual MK's case of breast cancer was, the cancer might not have been found until it had progressed much further. To MK's nurse's eye, MK had been granted a miracle.

And eventually, MK began to see it that way, too. Not an easy miracle. Not one she was seeking. Not one she would have signed up for. And not one that she's shoehorning into tidy theology. Nope. This is messy stuff. She says, "Here's what I'm not gonna do. I'm not gonna make light of the unexpected, tragic, baffling things that have happened in your life. I don't want to turn your hurt and your questions into some cheesy Hallmark card filled with pastel puppies and platitudes."

But she follows it up by saying,

> When things get sideways, and God seems more invisible than ever, you can trust this truth: He is still at work. In the doctor's office, the divorce attorney's office, and in the human resources office.
>
> He is still at work.
>
> You and I, we have to keep looking for it. We have to continue to search for His grace in the midst of our confusion. Sometimes, it feels like impossible work. But trust me, grace always shows up.

There is plenty of debate out there about how to pray and what it means if we don't receive what we pray for, and why we should pray at all. There aren't easy answers. Because life is messy, sometimes the answers are, too. But we can know this:

> *The LORD is near to all who call upon Him,*
> *To all who call upon Him in truth. (Psalm 145:18 NASB)*

And…

*I thank you that you have answered me
and have become my salvation. (Psalm 118:21 ESV)*

JOURNALING

What is something you've prayed for but haven't received?

....

....

....

....

....

What is the most irritating or tone-deaf thing someone has said
to you about a challenging situation in your life and prayer?

....

....

....

....

....

Have you had something in your life that initially seemed like a disaster but ended up being a miracle?

....

....

....

....

....

....

Write about something in your life that remains messy, even in the midst of prayers, even in the midst of seeking God. How are you living with the mess? What lessons have you learned as you wait to see what the outcome will be?

....

....

....

....

....

....

....

....

....

PRAYER

God, I want to be bold when I come to You in prayer. I confess it's sometimes hard for me to be bold because I don't want to pray for something that becomes a "gotcha." Help me, God, to know that there is power in the prayers I offer. And that You always have my good in mind. If there is something I'm praying for now for You to take away, let me lean into knowing You will do what is best. If there's something I'm missing praying for, by Your grace, fill in the gap. Thank You that You know how to take my prayers and answer them for my good, even when I don't realize the full ramifications of what I'm praying for. In Jesus' name, amen.

CHAPTER 4

SAND AND WATER

Our relationships with our physical bodies are convoluted at best. Depending on what stats you read, it's reported that 97 percent of women think on average thirteen negative thoughts about their bodies every day. And, weirdly, we sort of cheer this on. It's far more acceptable in our culture to belittle something about your figure, your face, or your fingernails than to say something you like about your physicality.

Another recent study revealed that almost 50 percent of girls between the ages of three and six were worried that they were fat. And the percentages of negative perspectives about their bodies keep climbing as girls grow older and become more aware of a culture that so often teaches us to judge one another and ourselves on our physical appearance.

MK writes about when she threw away a clay figure that her son made. To MK's eye, there was plenty to critique: The figurine, dubbed Little Man, was oddly shaped and sported a spooky expression. His disconcerting gaze seemed to follow MK as she worked around the kitchen. The experience was only heightened when her son mentioned that he and Little Man would sometimes have conversations. MK decided it was time for Little Man to hit the trash can. But she was in for a lesson in creator and creation when her son realized that Little Man was missing:

"Son, I'm sorry. I thought you were done with Little Man, so I threw him away. I'll help make a new one, if you want!"

Ben looked at me as if I'd kicked a puppy. Or worse, like I'd trashed his best friend. Which, I suppose, is exactly what I did. But, c'mon. Little Man was a clay thumb with googly eyes. Who could miss such a disaster?

"No," Ben replied, his eyes filling with tears. "I don't want another friend. I know he looked funny and his eyes were falling off, but he was the only Little Man in the world."

Thankfully, Ian, MK's husband, saw Little Man in the trash, thought he'd been tossed accidentally, and returned Little Man to his owner. MK's son was thrilled to get his misshapen friend back. As MK says, "I guess sometimes it's hard to see the beauty in something, unless you're the one that made it."

It may seem hard to believe at times, with our muffin tops, uncooperative pores, and split ends, but we are created in God's image. Precisely what that means has been the stuff of debates and heated discussions for millennia. But if we just take God's Word at its word, we can read it there in black and white: "So God created mankind in his own image, in the image of God he created them; male and female he created them" (Gen. 1:27 NIV). It's one thing to dislike the way your chin is shaped or the span of your hips. But what if you were to hear someone who looks like you or talks like you or laughs like you talk about how much they dislike themselves? And what if it was your child, a child you delighted over and thought was beautiful and special?

We toss out words about our bodies without a thought to the God who designed us after Himself. When we criticize ourselves, we criticize the Artist.

You may already be familiar with this incredible verse from Psalm 139:14: "I praise you, for I am fearfully and wonderfully made. Wonderful are your works; my soul knows it very well."

The Passion Translation says it this way: "I thank you, God, for making me so mysteriously complex! Everything you do is marvelously breathtaking. It simply amazes me to think about it! How thoroughly you know me, Lord!"

What if we started thinking of and seeing our physical bodies through the lens of God's incredible artistry and creation? What if we aligned what we said about ourselves and the physical creation that holds our souls on this earth with honoring the Artist and the One we are formed after?

Your body is built of 37.2 billion cells, somehow miraculously formed and held together by forces that can't even begin to be copied or fully understood. Even if you think it's shaped a little weird. Even if you're not crazy about the size of your thighs. Even if your culture has told you that your body doesn't measure up.

Watch what you say about you. Because the God who crafted you, the God who formed you, the God who thought through the details and the chromosomes and the cells that would make you *you*, He's listening. And He wants to hear you say what He says: that you are magnificent and a miracle.

JOURNALING
· · · · · · · · · · · · · · · · · ·

Is there a time that you've thrown something away, of your own or belonging to someone you love, and you later realized that you needed that item? What lengths have you taken to find the item or to replace it? What emotions did you experience in the process?

....

....

....

....

....

....

What messages did you receive growing up about your physical body?

....

....

....

....

....

....

Who do you think you most resemble in your biological family of origin?

....

....

....

....

What part of your body do you like the most? What is it you like about that part of your body?

....

....

....

....

What kinds of things do you say to your best friend about her physicality? What do you say to your children, nieces and nephews, or young people you mentor? Do you say the same things to yourself? Why or why not?

....

....

....

....

PRAYER
. . . .

Father, in all the things I wish were different in my life, in my body, in my relationships, in my today, in my past, help me never to forget that the dust that makes up the mess of me is beloved by You. Help me treasure it as a gift from You. Help me appreciate the marvel that it is, this incredible system of engineering and ingenuity and genius. And in appreciating it, help me not put too much focus on the physical body. You are my ultimate home; I know this body is a temporal gift for my immortal soul. Let me be thankful for it, and let me not overestimate it. Thank You for creating me in Your image. In the name of Jesus, amen.

CHAPTER 5

GHOSTS AND GUINEA PIGS

It starts out as a way to stave off boredom and ultimately becomes a paranormal crime investigation.

We're speaking, of course, about MK's fictional ghost, Charlie, and his fictional malevolent ways.

In her own life's take on *Stranger Things*, MK writes about the summer she convinced the other neighborhood kids that there was a ghost in their midst, the explanation for slammed doors, a variety of cat prey, and other mysterious happenings. Not only was a club of junior paranormal investigators convened, but there was also an official binder for keeping notes. The effort was all going swimmingly until a stray cat in the neighborhood began taking out all kinds of avian and rodent life and leaving it on the doorstep. At first, MK attributed these findings to Charlie the ghost, but as the body count kept climbing, her fellow ghost detectives began to become more and more freaked out, particularly her kid brother Ty. MK felt she was losing control of the story line but was saved from having to continue to cover for Charlie's antics when a neighbor began feeding the stray cat and the killings ceased.

But the mayhem wasn't over. When MK's brother's guinea pig died unexpectedly, MK started to think that her specter shenanigans were responsible for the guinea pig's demise. A confession to Momma and a call to the vet later, MK learned that she was exonerated because the guinea pig's death was due to loneliness. As it turns out, guinea pigs are a community kind of creature and do best when they have companionship.

Living in community is tricky for us as humans. Some of our biggest joys are within the context of family and friends. Some of our biggest hurts, regrets, and challenges are also within the context of our chosen community. We face potential rejection if we show up as who we truly are. If we come as ghosts of ourselves, wearing masks to conceal our vulnerability, we'll never be known. MK says:

The ghost of loneliness is making us crazy. We are out carving messages in trees. Except this time, the message is

"Please love me," and the tree is social media. I think the only thing that we want is to feel understood and seen. But the irony of all this specter building is that it's making us lonelier than ever.

You may think of loneliness as a state of being. But what if it's a symptom? If we're thirsty, we know the cure is to drink some water. If we're tired, we know the cure is sleep. Loneliness has its own cure as well. Psalm 68:6 says, "God sets the lonely in families, he leads out the prisoners with singing; but the rebellious live in a sun-scorched land" (NIV). Loneliness is not a condition to be lived with; it's a symptom with a cure. That's part of the beauty of how the church is supposed to function. "And if one member suffers, all the members suffer with it; if one member is honored, all the members rejoice with it," the apostle Paul tells us (1 Cor. 12:26 NASB). But the cure does come with the cost of focusing not only on our needs but also on the needs of others. And it does come with the risk of vulnerability.

Choosing to take the risk to be in community is the decision to do away with the ghost stories. The ghost stories about previous hurts and failures. The ghost stories we create about our lives only show up as the shining, tidy, polished versions of ourselves. We create these varieties of ghost stories out of one thing, says MK:

It's fear, y'all. Plain and simple. The scariest story you've ever heard is the one you are telling yourself: that if you are honest with people and share your flaws, they'll realize you are unlovable. Insecurity is haunting you and terrifying your town, but you don't have to believe it.

Do you want more connection in your life? Start by asking yourself what you believe about friendship and community. Are there ghost stories you're telling yourself? Do you believe you're worthy of relationships? Remember, there was no real Charlie the ghost menace in MK's childhood neighborhood; the menace was in her own mind. A good ghost story may have its place, but not in building a healthy community around you.

JOURNALING
· · · · · · · · · · · · · · · · · ·

"L.M.R.I.P., it said. That meant 'Let me rest in peace.'" This was the carving MK scratched into the tree outside her house that began the whole Charlie the ghost saga. Is there something in your life that you need to "let rest in peace"? Is there a wrong that was done to you in the past that continues to dominate your thoughts today?

....

....

....

....

....

MK goes on to write that what we've carved into that tree is "Please love me." What is something that you've done in the name of wanting to be loved that isn't true to who you are?

....

....

....

....

....

....

Do you sometimes let the ghosts of your past (e.g., former friendships gone wrong, betrayals, disappointment with people) color your sense of community? Why or why not?

....

....

....

....

What is your personality style? Do you find that you are energized by being around other people? Or do you find that while you enjoy people, you recharge when you have alone time? How does this impact your experience of community?

....

....

....

....

What was a time in your life when you were lonely? How did that sense of loneliness impact your overall sense of wellness?

....

....

....

....

What is a belief you've long had about yourself that you're now beginning to see might not be serving you well?

....

....

....

....

PRAYER

God, in those seasons where I find myself feeling lonely, let me turn to You first. Keep me from seeking the things that aren't good for me when I'm searching for a way to soothe my loneliness. Show me where I am making compromises that aren't healthy in my attempts to avoid being alone. Show me where I am avoiding friendships and connections in an attempt to prevent getting hurt. Make me brave to take the risk of being alone for a season to remove myself from relationships that aren't healthy, and make me brave to open myself up to relationships that You have for my good. In the name of Jesus, amen.

CHAPTER 6

WELCOME TO CHURCH, EVERYONE'S WEIRD HERE

L et's face it, church can be one of the messiest places.

Not the building. We Christians seem to take a great deal of pride in creating beautiful facilities in which to meet, complete with everything from exquisite stained glass windows to the latest high-def LED wall, depending on our preferred church aesthetic. No, we don't seem to have a problem in getting the venue right.

But that's not the church. The church is the people. And where there are people, there's always the potential for predicaments and perplexity and getting into pickles.

Messy, messy, messy.

MK confesses that she's felt out of place in church for most of her life and that, despite loving Jesus deeply, she finds that she feels weird when she's with the body of Christ, His church. She says, "For years, I would leave church every Sunday both inspired and incredibly frustrated. Inspired because people make the church beautiful. Frustrated because they also make it messy. These feelings were further complicated by the fact I'd show up thinking the body of Christ should be easy."

While already feeling a little awkward at church, MK's experiences take another turn during the Christmas season when her young daughter shares a medically accurate term about how Jesus was born, and MK has to meet with the Sunday school teacher in the aftermath of that revelation. It leaves MK feeling frustrated and embarrassed until a friend reminds her that most of us come to church looking for the same things: community, encouragement, and truth.

Carry each other's burdens, and in this way you will fulfill the law of Christ. (Galatians 6:2 NIV)

Maybe you're in a season where you feel like you've found just the right fit in a faith community. Or perhaps you feel like you've been on a never-ending search to find "your people." It's not wrong to want to find connection, people in the same age and stage of life, to sit in the pew alongside those who believe much like you do and share the same outlook on issues. But church is rarely like that because people are seldom in the same season with the same opinions and perspectives.

Church may be complicated for you. It may be the source of deep confusion, conflicting disappointment, and unmet expectations. MK says:

> I'm not downplaying this struggle. Heck, I had to start and restart this chapter because I would get a few hundred words in and then realize that I was ranting about church, rather than celebrating and accepting its messiness. You feel it too, right? You've volunteered for all the things. You've had leaders disappoint you. You've fallen in love with a church, and then you've seen the underbelly of how things are run. It makes *you* want to run. I understand.
>
> So why do we even mess with it?

In spite of the challenges of meeting together as a group of believers, the writer of Hebrews reminds us, "And let us consider how we may spur one another on toward love and good deeds, not giving up meeting together, as some are in the habit of doing, but encouraging one another—and all the more as you see the

Day approaching" (10:24–25 NIV). We usually focus on that part about not giving up meeting together, but let's not miss this: There were those in the early church who *were* giving up on it. It makes you wonder if, even in those early days of the church, while it was practically still in the honeymoon period, there were already those who were finding it hard to deal with the messiness of church life.

As MK asks, why should we even mess with it?

Because somehow, in embracing the messiness, we find cleansing. MK writes:

> But something wild happens when you consistently hang out with a motley crew of believers. Community has this bizarrely cleansing effect. It helps us move past our selfishness. It stretches our ability to love. Church leaves no room for the fantasy that people of faith have it all together.

God can show up anywhere, at any time. He's not constrained by our ideas of schedules and service flows. But scripture also says that God is there when believers huddle up: "For where two or three gather in my name, there I am with them" (Matt. 18:20 NIV).

Church will never be perfect. What seems an ideal fit today might change tomorrow. A place you could never see yourself attending might become your new church home. Church as we know it scribbles outside the lines, points fingers, and throws temper tantrums. It's messy, dynamic, and filled with people who are at different places in their lives, with different opinions, politics, perspectives, and personalities.

And it's family. A big, boisterous, dysfunctional family that God claims as His own.

JOURNALING
· · · · · · · · · · · · · · · · · ·

Where are you in your church life today?

....

....

....

....

What changed for you during the pandemic in your church community?

....

....

....

....

If you could change something about your current church life, what would it be?

....

....

....

....

....

Why do you think God wants us to have a faith community?

....

....

....

....

....

Have you ever felt shamed by someone in your immediate faith community? What happened?

....

....

....

....

....

Do you find yourself feeling inspired by your time at church but also frustrated?

....

....

....

....

....

PRAYER

Father, I know church, the collection of people who come together in Your name, is an essential experience in helping me understand the mystery of Your kingdom. I confess there are times church as a social gathering or produced experience has become more important than serving. I confess there are times my patience with the practice of church has become thin. I confess there are times I'm embarrassed by how people behave in the name of the church. I confess there are times it would be simpler not to subject myself to it. Give me the patience to see the power of gathering in Your name. Give me the maturity to see beyond the man-made minutiae. Give me the grace to be part of this flicker of Your kingdom on earth known as the church. In the name of Jesus, amen.

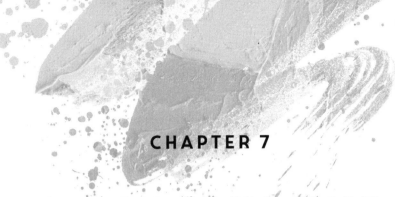

CHAPTER 7

ON SHARKS AND THERAPISTS

People are scary.

Some are scary because they try to be. They want to appear domineering, intimidating, powerful. They put on the trappings to fulfill that image, from clothing that makes them look tough to accessories that make them look rich to attitudes that overwhelm the masses.

And then there are people who are scary simply because they are…people. People who we might disappoint. People who might disappoint us. People who might leave us or misunderstand us, or discover our darkest thoughts.

Those people are scary too.

We're told to be afraid of the bogeyman, but what happens when we start to see almost everyone in our world as dangerous?

MK recounts her philosophy that therapists can be some of the scariest people of all. "This is because, as gentle and whispery as they are," she writes, "therapists have an affinity for Jedi mind tricks. You take a seat in their office, feeling pretty good about life, and next thing you know you're sobbing about that boy in sixth grade who called you a rottweiler because you were the only girl who wasn't shaving yet."

It dawns on MK that her therapist may be just as afraid of her as she is of him. Just as MK's dad told her years before that sharks and snakes and all manner of scary things are just as scared of you as you are of them, MK realizes that it could be true of people as well.

It's an instinct you can observe with animals in nature. When they feel afraid or threatened, they'll probably do one of two things: try to make themselves appear bigger or shrink back to get as small as possible, to draw less attention to themselves. And you and I may do the same thing as well.

Someone comes at us in anger? Maybe we match their volume and tone in response.

Or maybe we pull back, acquiesce, make ourselves small.

Feeling awkward in a new situation with people you don't know? Prime time for shrinking.

As MK ponders this idea, that her therapist might be just as scared of her, that we all are probably tempted to show ourselves as less than we are, she discovers this verse:

I take no pleasure in the one who shrinks back. (Hebrews 10:38 NIV)

She says about this verse, "I'll tell you what I believe. It means raising our voice when it comes to the things that matter. Taking our steps in confidence when we know we are walking with God. It means that we don't retreat to our safe little shells when our messiness makes us feel vulnerable. God relishes those who don't shrink away, because He created us for a bold life."

Maybe you have believed that your job was to try to fit in with as many people as possible, to be as neutral and vanilla as needed to move through the groups of people in your life without so much as a ripple. Maybe you were even taught that was the mark of a "good" Christian, someone who never made waves, never drew attention to themselves, never stood out. Maybe you've been living like your job is to never give anyone any reason to ever reject you.

What if that's not necessarily true?

"The hard truth is this: Rejection is part of the human experience," MK shares. "In a world as wildly diverse as this one, it's not possible to fit in at every table. But the good news is, you don't have to. I'm serious about this. Please hear me. It's not your responsibility to tone yourself down so you can fit in at somebody else's table. I'll wait a minute while you read that a few more times."

Maybe, just maybe, it's time to turn up the volume on all God created you to be.

JOURNALING

What creatures in nature are you most afraid of? Snakes, sharks, spiders, vultures, bats, cockroaches? Why?

....

....

....

Who have you been "scared" of in your life because you thought they had it all together and would never be interested in someone like you? What did you ultimately learn about that person? Did they end up being far more down-to-earth than you imagined? Did they grapple with self-worth or confidence that seemed at odds with who you thought they were? What happened as you got to know them better?

....

....

....

Where in your life do you find that you tend to shrink back?

....

....

....

"The tragic irony of trying to conform to the world by lessening who we are is that in an effort to avoid society's rejection, we are rejecting the very people that God created us to be," writes MK. What light that God gifted you with have you been hiding? What are you going to do to change that?

....

....

....

....

....

....

....

To you, where is the line between being who you were created to be versus putting yourself, your preferences, and your needs above everyone else's? What does a balanced approach to fully being yourself *and* living selflessly look like? Who does that well in your world?

....

....

....

....

PRAYER

There are times, Lord, when I play too small and shrink back from who You have created me to be in an attempt to fit in. And there are times when I let my preferences and agenda overshadow the other needs around me. Show me how to live in the tension of being true to myself while also being true to others. Remind me that people are just as scared of being rejected by me as I am of being rejected by them. Help me become a safe harbor for the scared, the disenfranchised, and those who feel unseen. In the name of Jesus I pray, amen.

CHAPTER 8

TWO TRUTHS AND A LIE

The lies we believe about ourselves, our worth, our likability, and our "lovability" don't always appear as obvious falsehoods.

Often lies take a far more devious and calculating approach.

There's a type of wasp called the *Glyptapanteles* that uses an insidious method to keep its species going. It finds an innocent little caterpillar and injects its eggs into it. From the outside, the caterpillar continues to look normal. But a day comes when the wasp eggs develop into larvae and, in a true horror-movie-worthy moment, begin to chew through the skin of the caterpillar in a macabre moment of birth.

It's gross. Fascinating. But gross.

That's how lies can operate in our lives. A lie will find a host, something that we know to be true, and inject its seeping poison. And before we know it, we allow something that is a truth in our lives to morph into something completely other.

A bad grade on a math quiz becomes the lie that we are stupid.

A day we're feeling bloated becomes the lie that no one will ever find us attractive.

A struggle we're experiencing becomes the lie of total identity.

MK recounts her experience with this kind of odious math. She tells of two truths: one, that she had a hard time making friends as a kid; and two, that she was still struggling with making friends today. Combined, it allowed those two truths to become the lie that she was unlovable. She says, "A wound can seem so small and harmless at first, but if it's ignored and untreated? Well, even the tiniest opening can allow something more nefarious to slip in."

You may have some hard truths in your life. And sometimes, you might think that the way to get past the lies in your life is to ignore the truths. But a rejection, an embarrassment, a mess-up, or a hurt doesn't go away simply because we decide to ignore it or act like it never happened. MK says, "Nothing that bruises us is silly or insignificant. And Satan will try to use all of it. He will take your hurtful history, your distrust, your doubt, and spin some masterfully calculated lies." Recognizing and owning the truths in your life, even the tough ones, is important. What you do next with the equation determines whether you will learn from those truths and heal or if you will allow those truths to be used as a weapon against you.

How do we get past this type of arithmetic, the kind that would have us believing that we are less than what God created us to be, that we are locked into a loop of unlovability or continual failure? God math looks a little different than yours and mine. Proverbs 3:5–6 says, "Trust in the LORD with all your heart, and do not lean on your own understanding. In all your ways acknowledge him, and he will make straight your paths" (ESV). Our understanding of how the events and challenges and wounds in our lives add up doesn't necessarily line up with God's plan.

God isn't confused; He's quantum. He knows we're a mess. He knows we go through some messes. He knows we're going to make a mess, and some people will try to make a mess out of us.

But the truth of our mess doesn't change the truth of His message. He's got these Post-it notes stuck everywhere for you and me, which remind us of a higher truth and a sum total greater than all our messy parts.

Therefore, if anyone is in Christ, he is a new creation.
The old has passed away; behold, the new has come.
(2 Corinthians 5:17 ESV)

For we are his workmanship, created in Christ Jesus for good works, which God prepared beforehand, that we should walk in them. (Ephesians 2:10 ESV)

There is therefore now no condemnation for those who are in Christ Jesus. (Romans 8:1 ESV)

JOURNALING

What are two truths that have led you to believe a lie?

....

....

....

....

When do you first remember identifying these truths? And when did you first notice that the combination of these two truths led you to a conclusion about yourself?

....

....

....

....

As you think about this conclusion, ask yourself: Is my conclusion true? Why or why not?

....

....

....

....

Does your conclusion line up with what God says about you?

....

....

....

....

Write a new equation here. Take a couple of truths, add them together, and then check your homework against what God says about you. Write it out:

$$\begin{array}{l} \;\text{...} \\ +\;\text{...} \\ =\;\text{...} \end{array}$$

Answer Key: "In all these things we are more than conquerors through him who loved us" (Rom. 8:37 ESV).

PRAYER

Father, help me identify the lies among the truths in my life. I might struggle to believe that lies could be hiding there, but I want to make sure I'm living fully in who You say I am instead of being at risk of harboring something You don't want for me. Show me where my math is off in how I understand my life and the purpose You have for me. And by the power of Your Holy Spirit, help me become more and more adept at spotting when the enemy is trying to weave in falsehood. Make me better at spotting his schemes, before they create damage and confusion. Thank You for being the God of truth. In the name of Jesus, amen.

CHAPTER 9

FIND YOUR FELLOW GOAT THIEVES

t starts early, this desire to fit in with the "It Crowd," to be validated by those who seem to have influence, looks, and popularity. Some people seem to be welcomed to the cool kids' table from earliest days.

And then there are the rest of us mere mortals.

Community is a big buzzword these days. In our workplaces, our neighborhoods, and our churches, the idea of community, its importance and its necessity, seems to be on a loop. And we get it. Yes, life is sweeter, healthier, and more faceted when we have community.

But what happens when the group you want to have community with doesn't seem to want it with you? It can feel like you're back in those awkward school days, longing to be accepted by the group that defines the most gleaming and glamorous example of community, but finding yourself on the outside, always looking in.

MK writes about her attempts to become part of the popular circle, her failed campaign running for class president, and the variety of ways she seemed to miss out on friend groups. That began to change when she tried something different. Instead of pursuing a particular group, she accepted an invitation to play drums in a band in middle school. It was a group of kids she might not have thought to hang out with before. But ultimately, she learns that this new circle of friends are the ones who have her back, even when dealing with the consequences of MK's adventures in a dramatic (and upholstery-destroying) rescue.

She says, "You have to stop chasing relationships with people whose circle is closed. Maybe they are too distracted with their lives to make room for a new relationship. Maybe they are in a social funk, or maybe they simply don't get you. That's not on you, my friend. Don't you dare water yourself down to be palatable for others. You are freaking fabulous—find a circle that sees it."

When building a group of friends, it's understandable that we might first look to those who stand out to us, who seem to have lots of friends. We might interpret that level of influence as evidence that a person knows how to be a great friend. And maybe they do. But the size of someone's friend group doesn't always mean they've got the community thing figured out. Proverbs 18:24 says, "A man of many companions may come to ruin, but there is a friend who sticks closer than a brother" (ESV). It raises the question, what are you looking for in developing a community? Do you want a handful of people who stand by you, pray for you, show up and laugh, and help you rehome an abused goat (or whatever other adventure has your name on it)?

Or...are you looking for a group that you think will help you wash away the things you don't like about yourself, a collection of people who make you feel validated because of their status, education, tax bracket, or notoriety? That kind of community will most likely not be the one that is there for the long haul because it's built on the shaky base of shaky self-worth. And at the first slight, the first inconvenience, it could come crashing down.

Maybe it's time to look in different places than you have before for the people who can become your people. They might not be your same age. They might not have the same life experiences. They might have different opinions and be at a different point in their faith walk.

And they might just be for you.

It takes vulnerability and risk to try and try again to create the circle that you'll experience life with. Not all people are meant to be your people. Not every group that finds connection needs to add more members. What matters is that you open yourself to seeing who God will bring into your life. No angling to get in with the cool kids. No need to be seen as an "It Girl."

The rewards can be sweet. "I had found *my people*," writes MK. "The ones who would never hide behind the azaleas. Who saw my weird and thought it was wonderful. Who reciprocated vulnerability, support, and unconditional love. They were my partners in crime, and my fellow goat thieves. They were more than worth the wait."

How do you know when you've found your people? It should feel a little something like this:

Sweet friendships refresh the soul and awaken our hearts with joy, for good friends are like the anointing oil that yields the fragrant incense of God's presence. (Proverbs 27:9 TPT)

JOURNALING
· · · · · · · · · · · · · · · · · ·

Who were the popular kids when you were in school? Did you feel like you were part of that group? Why or why not?

....

....

....

....

....

....

....

Why do you think you identify some people as popular and others as not? For you, does it have to do with prestige, talent, position, and connections?

....

....

....

....

....

....

....

The popular kids' phenomenon doesn't stop once we leave our school days. Workplaces, churches, and social groups still have their token golden child. What do you notice about the people in your adult world who seem to be at the center of community circles?

....

....

....

....

....

....

Who surprised you by becoming your friend? How are they different from your other friends? What drew you to them?

....

....

....

....

....

....

....

....

PRAYER

God, I confess there are times that I want to be seen and accepted by the "sparkly" people, the ones who seemingly have the attention of others, who have prestige and influence. And sometimes, I seek to intercept circles of friends and run the risk of making my acceptance by that circle something of an idol in my life. Please give me eyes to see the friendships possible with people You place in my life. Open my heart to discovering friendships with those who know how to celebrate me in the areas where I'm strong, in the areas where I'm weak, in the areas where I'm assured, and in the areas where I feel needy. Forgive me when I have missed an opportunity brought by You to add an amazing person to my life. And please bring me friendships that bring me closer to You. In the name of Jesus, amen.

CHAPTER 10

ANNIVERSARY RATS

It's hard to believe. But there is no anniversary that corresponds to the gift of a rat. Paper, yes. Silver, uh-huh. Flowers, candy, copper? Check, check, and check.

Rodents?

No, no, and heck no.

But that's exactly what MK received from her husband, Ian, on their anniversary.

It went about as well as you might imagine. As in, not well at all.

In the tumult and conflict that resulted, MK demands that they return to their premarital counselors to help them get back on track. Whereupon she discovers that their premarital counselors have gotten a divorce.

Weddings, honeymoons, anniversaries, and the daily grind of building a life together sometimes result in rats instead of rainbows and puppies and butterflies. Our ideas about what romance should look like can result in frustration and hurt. Why? As MK explains, "Some of our biggest messes are born in the collision of reality and expectation."

Expectations build over time. From our earliest days, we gather messages about what relationships are supposed to look like, what a partner is supposed to be like, and what adoration and devotion are supposed to feel like. From Disney princess love stories to *Twilight*-esque drama to *Pride and Prejudice* witty banter, the notions about love and courtship and longing and enchantment surround us everywhere we look. And not all of the messages we pick up on are bad or unrealistic; after all, if you've got a set of grandparents in your life who have been married over fifty years and still dance to "their" song every evening after dinner and who still get teary every time they retell the story of how they met, then you've got baked into your history a really high expectation setting, a bar set on full-dial. Of course, that idealistic grandparent kind of love probably also has experienced its own challenges, but, understandably, that's a facet you probably haven't seen. And when those expectations, Disney-made or cute-grandparent-built, come standing alongside what your life and love look like, your hoped-for happy can turn to havoc.

But MK reminds us that there is something vital we must do when it comes to looking at our own relationship and what we think it should be:

> And the only way you will survive that mess is if you remove the bars someone else set. Notice that I didn't say to lower the bar. I'm just saying *know who set it*. There are some ideals that no human can meet. And those expectations only cause trouble.

Perhaps we should be aiming for a relationship that is strong instead of the Hallmark movie kind of romance. Strong in bond, strong in connection, and especially strong in an ingredient that, when given in generous measure by both parties, can get you through a whole lot of mess. "The strongest relationships hold space for the messes and can offer grace for each other's imperfections," says MK.

Beyond love languages and anniversary gifts is a present that can change the dynamics of your relationship. It will cost you, but it also has the potential of being extended to you when you need it. Jesus says in Matthew 5:7, "Blessed are the merciful, for they shall receive mercy" (NASB). You may experience times when it seems like the magic and flutters that marked the beginning of your relationship have ended. You may be more irritated with your partner than you are in sync.

But any long-term romantic relationship requires copious amounts of expectation-adjustment, grace and mercy, and forgiveness. Make no mistake; the enemy would love to have you stewing on all manner of shortcomings in your spouse. As the saying goes, what you look at and focus on tends to grow. But the opposite is also true. Proverbs 17:9 says, "Love prospers when a fault is forgiven, but dwelling on it separates close friends" (NLT). The idea that love is not static, that it can grow and flourish, even over time, and kids and mortgages and, yes, disastrous anniversary gifts, is a source of hope that doesn't often get covered in our microwaved romantic media of today.

Your marriage?

It's the long game. And maybe, just maybe, it would do us all good to let the mascot be the anniversary rat, a reminder that love is messy. That's part of the mystery and joy.

JOURNALING
· · · · · · · · · · · · · · · · · ·

What is the weirdest gift you've received? What was the occasion, and how did it make you feel?

....

....

....

What kind of wedding and marriage did you think you would have? What set that bar for you?

....

....

....

....

What has surprised you the most in your dating experiences or your marriage experience? Why do you think it was surprising to you? Did you feel unprepared, or did you think you would do things differently than some of the cautionary tales around you?

....

....

....

....

Write about a time you needed a lot of grace in your relationship. What were some of the factors that played into your behavior? What did you learn from the experience?

....

....

....

....

....

....

Are there expectations set in faith communities about romance and love and marriage that you feel are not helpful? What are they? What do you think would be more beneficial for couples?

....

....

....

....

....

....

....

....

....

PRAYER
· · · · · · · · · ·

Romantic love and marriage is a picture of how You love the church and Your people, God, the metaphor You have used to explain the connection of Christ and the church. But there can be such deep hurt and misunderstanding in marriage, in romance. Father, help me understand the relationship You have created for my partner and me. Show me how to take the wisdom of those who have navigated relationships, but don't let me forget that You have made me unique and my partner unique, which means we will have a unique romance. Help me release the expectations that don't serve us well, the expectations that become the catalyst for conflict. Strengthen our bond, strengthen our understanding, and most importantly, strengthen our desire to extend and receive mercy and grace from each other. In Jesus' name, amen.

CHAPTER 11

BAGGAGE CLAIM

Reunions. It seems a slightly masochistic rite of passage in adulthood to go back to your high school or college years and reconnect with your friends from that era. Sometimes it might be for bragging rights; the high school kid nobody noticed has undergone some dramatic glow-up in physical beauty or bank account, and they splash into the local hotel ballroom for the ten-year reunion unrecognizable and beaming with a sense of *Gotcha!*

Sometimes reunions are for sipping from the gilded cup of the glory days, when life seemed easier. Sometimes they're for trying to recapture a young adulthood peak. And hopefully, at their best, reunions are a time to reconnect with old friends.

Whatever the reasons for reunion-ing, you can be sure there

will probably be a bit of mess in its wake, whether it's regrets reborn, melancholy, prickly pride, memories awakened, comparison, or smugness.

When you circle back to visit times and past seasons, you'll bring some baggage. History has its own set of luggage, and no matter how tidily we pack up the experiences of our pasts, there's bound to be some in-flight leakage.

MK discovers a lot of unfinished business sloshing around in her carry-on when she receives an invitation to a cheerleading reunion, her "cheerunion." She'd skipped the last one but decided not only to attend this one but to host it at her family's lake house. Many IBS symptoms, doubts, and upsets later, MK packs her bags, heads to the lake house, and waits for her fellow cheerleaders to arrive, people who, to MK's memory, made her last year of high school simply awful.

The emotional baggage gets unpacked during a late-night gab session at the lake house. MK asks why her fellow cheer friends, back in the day, had petitioned to have MK removed as the cheer captain. The reunion gals apologize for the hurt MK has been packing all this time but also explain that MK's seeming distraction from the cheer squad and her absence from attending an important training camp precipitated the petition. MK then reveals that during that time, she was testifying against her stepfather in court about the sexual abuse she experienced from him, something her fellow cheerleaders didn't know.

There's something so powerful when baggage bursts open with the right people at the right time. MK writes, "And then, something happened, that to this day breaks me in the best possible way. One by one, the women got up and walked over to my chair. They huddled around me, wrapped me in love, and together, we cried healing tears."

What we carry greatly impacts how we perceive our lives, our pasts, and the people who populate those landscapes. MK's horrific baggage about what she suffered with her stepfather led to the misunderstanding of her cheer squad. A decade later, the baggage was unpacked. And healing resulted.

Too often, we carry for far too long what we weren't meant to carry alone. "Turn your burdens over to the LORD," says Psalm 55:22, "and he will take care of you" (GW). When the items in our baggage stay hidden in the dark, they develop more barbs and razor-sharp edges, slicing us from the inside when we bump up against triggers and memories on the outside. But in those moments when we stand among our fellow travelers in life, who are also lugging their own luggage behind them, and we acknowledge we're all standing there with our messy stuff stuffed into the fragile containers of our hearts, healing can happen. Hope can show up.

A new chapter begins, and a new day dawns when we lighten the load we carry.

I removed the burden from their shoulders; their hands were set free from the basket. (Psalm 81:6–7 NIV)

JOURNALING

Write about a time when you underwent tremendous heartache but kept it concealed from those around you.

....

....

....

What is something that you've been surprised you're still carrying? Is it a hurt from elementary school or a comment made years ago by a friend or a parent? What happens when that memory comes popping up?

....

....

....

....

Why do you think you hold on to some of your baggage?

....

....

....

....

Sometimes the baggage we haul around is something that was handed to us, like family of origin dynamics or a cause that someone has recruited us to. As you think about this baggage, is it something you could put down? Is there baggage you have carried for someone else? Why or why not?

....

....

....

....

Write about a time you decided to leave some emotional baggage behind. What did you experience? Did it feel like a relief, or did it feel scary?

....

....

....

....

PRAYER
. . . .

Many times in Your Word, Father, You tell me I can hand off the burdens and baggage of this life. But certain chapters in my memory, particularly hurts, continue to haunt and wound me. I want to hand them to You, God. I want to walk in the light burden that Jesus talks about instead of the crushing weight of regret and misunderstanding. But I don't always know how to do it, how to set the heaviness down and walk away. And my emotions often don't seem to go along with that plan. Help me to heal. Help me to let go. Help me to forgive others and myself so that I can walk with more lightness and joy. I pray this in the name of Jesus, amen.

CHAPTER 12

BIRTH IS A MESSY AFFAIR

Coming into a new season of life, starting a new job, launching out on your own, beginning a new relationship, dropping habits that haven't served you, reaching for a new friend group, and moving into a new level in your spirituality are all types of birthing.

And they're all going to be messy.

No matter how anesthetized and orderly we try to make the birth process for anything, be it a new endeavor or a new kid, there's going to be some splash.

We can be especially guilty of thinking we can tidy up the birth process when it comes to our spiritual lives. Have you ever been part of one of those "Cardboard Testimonies" services at church?

It's an HGTV-reno-reality-show kind of approach to redemption and change on the soul level, all wrapped up in a specific time block before the sermon. You roll out with your sin on one side of a cardboard sign, something like, "Our marriage was failing," or "I was secretly drinking too much." There are fellow presenters alongside you, each with their own cardboard signs listing their transgressions and challenges. You give everyone in the congregation a chance to read what your situation was, along with your fellow presenters. And then, as the praise and worship music swells, you and your cardboard-sign buddies flip your signs on cue.

And there, on the reverse side of each of those pieces of cardboard, is the "after."

"Our marriage is better than ever!"

"I haven't had a drink in thirty-two days!"

The congregation members applaud and get to their feet. The band plays out the refrain of the music. And everyone leaves feeling encouraged.

But then there's the next day. And that marriage that was doing great encounters a bump. And that bottle that has been ignored starts rattling.

Why? Because birth is messy. It can't be contained within the borders of a rectangle of cardboard. And it seems to MK that's the whole reason Jesus used birth language when talking about what it is like to follow Him:

In biblical times, there were no birthing centers or Caribbean dolphin deliveries. There were no epidurals or constant monitors, no tests that could mitigate risk. The crowd that was gathered at the temple that day knew nothing of modern medicine. They had never seen a Hollywood movie where the baby came out pink and perfect. Those who were gathered knew labor and suffering—the messiest side of childbirth. And yet Jesus told them, in the plainest of terms, that their spirits must be *reborn*.

We crave fast-and-easy before-and-after stories when it comes to our faith journeys. Not only that, we tend to think something is wrong when those journeys get messy. We discover that someone we thought had a "true" conversion is grappling with sin. We hear that someone "delivered" from a challenge is fighting it again. We are surprised and wonder among ourselves if they didn't fully "surrender" to God, if that's why things have gone a little sloppy.

But even the apostle Paul, he of the staunch opinions and debate background, even he encountered the messy and ongoing birth process of becoming more like Jesus. In Romans 7:15–17, he says, "I'm a mystery to myself, for I want to do what is right, but end up doing what my moral instincts condemn. And if my behavior is not in line with my desire, my conscience still confirms the excellence of the law. And now I realize that it is no longer my true self doing it, but the unwelcome intruder of sin in my humanity" (TPT).

What kind of grace could we give ourselves and give to others if we were more clear about the first-century birth conditions to which Jesus was making an analogy? What if we embraced that birth is a messy affair? What if we continued to push (pun intended) toward the good but also recognized that growth and change and development aren't always linear?

JOURNALING
· · · · · · · · · · · · · · · · · ·

If you've given birth, what surprised you most about the process? Or, if you haven't given birth but have seen videos or been with someone birthing, what stands out to you about labor and delivery?

....

....

....

....

....

....

Do you love before-and-after content, home renovations, fitness stories, or makeup tutorials? What draws you to that type of content?

....

....

....

....

....

....

There are times when we can experience a pretty instantaneous before-and-after in our walk with Jesus. Is there something in your spiritual journey that has felt that way?

....

....

....

....

....

....

Is there something you've been fighting to overcome, such as a mindset, habit, or sin cycle? Why do you think that process has been longer and more challenging? Does it encourage you to rethink the redemption birth process, to consider that it can be messy and full of starts and stops and starts? Why or why not?

....

....

....

....

....

....

....

PRAYER

Father, I want the messes in my life to be cleaned up quickly, for You to sweep in like a crack housekeeping unit and clear all the grime. And I know that when it comes to forgiveness, You do that for me instantly. But give me the patience and the courage to walk out the rest of the birthing process, to work through the disciplines and changes that honor the forgiveness You extend. Let me have that same patience and courage with those around me who are also in birthing rooms of their own, with the sights, sounds, and smells of the birth process that don't always match the way I think it should be. Let me behold both the wonder and the messiness of being born again in holy awe. In the name of Jesus, amen.

CHAPTER 13

THE MAGIC OF THE MOON

There are elements of magic in childhood that we want to extend for as long as we can. We aim to protect kids from some of the world's tougher realities, insulating them from the ache and spitting gravel kicked up by the sharp brass tacks of life.

It's not always possible.

MK's family of origin was split by divorce when she was five years old. It ended certain enchanting beliefs she held and how she saw the world. No matter her mother's gentle guidance through this season, it was impossible to buffer the impact of such an event. MK says:

One of the hardest things a mother must do is teach the language of pain. To give her child a word for divorce, or cancer, or death. A word that doesn't give life to something beautiful but, rather, sucks life out of something beautiful. I remember learning one such word that forever altered my universe. Big fat tears streamed down my cheeks as Momma explained divorce. It was a word that told me love was impermanent, and grief could be felt for the living.

And life became more complicated and dark when MK's mother remarried, and the man who became MK's stepfather began sexually abusing her.

It all left MK with a sense that the things that should have been miraculous, including God, had failed her.

Watching your childhood or your marriage or your family or your faith burn down can leave you with very little innocent wonder left for the world. Just like when Dorothy realizes that the World of Oz that has initially left her filled with awe is all the conjuring of a simpering and concealing mortal, it can feel like a necessary survival skill to drop your marvel and replace it with sage cynicism.

It's after MK becomes friends with Brian in college, a guy who follows Jesus in a tender way, that she rediscovers a connection with God. She says,

> There's something available to you and me, we who journey through messes in life. We have access to an authentic innocence through God, a restoration of trust. No matter what we've seen or what we've experienced, there is peace when we come to our Father. We can be childlike before Him, asking our questions, letting Him heal and hold us. It's okay to not have all the answers. It's okay to not understand everything. It's okay to admit we are tired of drifting and we long for some hope to ground us.

Trust that has been broken through broken marriages and relationships, broken dreams, or broken hope can find its way home. The writer of Psalm 56:3–4 penned, "When I am afraid, I put my trust in you. In God, whose word I praise, in God I trust; I shall not be afraid" (ESV). Because, at the end of the day, struggling to trust finds its basis in fear, being afraid of being hurt again, being afraid of being caught off guard like we were in the initial hurt. The healing balm for broken trust starts with acknowledging the fear and asking for God's help in combating it.

We can be restored to seeing the wonder, beauty, and awe of

life when we can look at our existence through His eyes instead of the jaded haze of hurt. Maybe that's why we are so often referred to in Scripture as God's children. After all, Jesus tells us that there are things that only children, through childlike faith, can see and understand about the magnitude and the mystery of the kingdom of God: "At that time Jesus said, 'I praise you, Father, Lord of heaven and earth, because you have hidden these things from the wise and learned, and revealed them to little children'" (Matt. 11:25 NIV).

It's not childish to see the good; it's childlike. It's not naive to respond to beauty with wonder. It's not unsophisticated to giggle, skip, and play; it's wholehearted. God still sees you as His child, and there are still childlike qualities that are yours to have.

JOURNALING

What is something that you found magic in as a child, something that was delightful and mysterious?

....

....

....

....

....

....

....

What is something that you discovered as you were growing up that took some of the wonder out of your world? How did that peek behind the scenes impact you?

....

....

....

....

....

....

....

Write about a time in your adult life when you also discovered that something was different than what you initially thought it was or the way it was presented. Was it a boss who was incredibly helpful and friendly during the interview process, only to become verbally abusive and difficult on the job? Was it a church group in which you thought you were accepted, only to discover there was intense gossip afoot? What was it for you, and how has it impacted how you look at things today?

....

....

....

....

....

MK writes about meeting Brian in college, a friend who would ultimately help in her journey to Jesus. Who is someone in your life who has lovingly walked with you in your faith journey? What do you notice about the way they have been there for you?

....

....

....

....

What has surprised you in your relationship with God? MK discovered a new way of understanding who God is to her; she needed a fresh perspective since the language about family and fathers meant abandonment and brokenness to her, not divine love. Where has God mended your understanding or healed your definition of things that have wounded you in the past?

PRAYER

God, I recognize that there are places where my heart has become hardened and jaded by things I have experienced and wounds I have received. And some of those things have influenced and changed how I look at You. Restore to me the ability to see You through a child's eyes. Make new my understanding of who You are, not impeded by the clutter of my years on this earth. Replace anything that has come into my heart that blocks my ability to see Your miraculous, unfathomable glory. Let me embrace in complete trust that I can rest in You as Your beloved child. In the name of Jesus I pray, amen.

CHAPTER 14

GUARDRAILS AND POOL NOODLES

When we open ourselves up to new love and attachment, we also open ourselves up to a big ball of possible heartache. MK reveals that her favorite character in the Lord of the Rings series is probably not the one people typically fangirl over. It's Gollum, the creepy, selfish, conflicted hobbit-turned-tortured-salamander-like creature who clutches a gold ring to his heart, uttering in a hissing whisper over and over the words "My Precious." MK says that she relates to Gollum because she herself has known the panic and paranoia that come with knowing what is most precious to you can be taken.

MK writes that when her first child was born and began to

crawl and toddle, her sense of terror became even more heightened. "Things got harder when Ben started to crawl—as moving children are harder to manage. So, I bought approximately eight thousand pool noodles and a few rolls of duct tape and covered every corner in the house," she writes. "To be honest, our living room looked like an asylum, which I guess was exactly the point. I had mitigated every possible risk. There was no hint of danger. No need for the whispers. I was miserable and lonely, but my son was alive. I was keeping him safe, *My Precious.*"

Ultimately her son's pediatrician gives MK this important reminder: "Growing up is a process of discovering corners. You can't prevent every boo-boo. It's a parent's job to babyproof the house and buckle their children in correctly. You are doing that very well. But accidents happen, and Ben will get hurt. It's going to break your heart. Some lessons in life leave bruises, and that's okay. Pain is an important teacher."

We don't like that line, that pain is an important teacher. But we also want the freedom to bump into things, to try this or that, to test the limits of what God shows us is good and healthy for us against what the world wants to serve up. We push back on Scripture, we think we've found a way no one has ever thought of before, and *BAM!*, we find the corner of the table with the edge of our chin. Writes MK, "There's this special shine, an air of intrigue, that surrounds anything off-limits. Since the Garden of

Eden, creation has shown that we want the things we can't have. Sin wouldn't tempt us if it tasted sour the moment it touched our tongue. Ask Eve how tasty that apple was, right up 'til it ruined her life."

God's Word says, "Now the Lord is the Spirit, and where the Spirit of the Lord is, there is freedom" (2 Cor. 3:17 NIV). So how does that freedom line up with what can sometimes feel like confining rules and regulations?

A big part of it has to do with how we receive that guidance of Scripture. MK says, "We are viewing the Bible as a collection of rules, when, in fact, it's our lifesaving guardrails." God knew we were going to head for the edges in our lives. He knew we would get banged up. And we prove Him right over and over.

Thankfully, that's not the end of the story. God's grace covers us when we bump into the corners. He uses the consequences we find there to move us closer to Him. And if we are willing to learn, rather than to lean away from Him, we can grow and remember that guardrails are for our good, not for limiting our lives, but for clearing the path to vibrant living.

JOURNALING

· · · · · · · · · · · · · · · · ·

Have you experienced a panic attack, or have you been with
someone who was having one? What did you notice about it?
What was the scariest part about it?

....

....

....

....

....

....

MK writes about her early days of motherhood and how she
found the fear that came with loving her baby so much became
incredibly overwhelming. Have you experienced that kind of
feeling before?

....

....

....

....

....

....

"One of the hardest things a person can do is heal their perception of Scripture. Most of us have experienced seasons in life in which we've fallen out of love with the Bible. Maybe you are in such a season now," writes MK. Where are you in your relationship to Scripture? Does it feel like a rule-studded weapon, or do you find yourself in a season of peace?

....

....

....

Write about a time you experienced the Word of God being used against you as a weapon of shame.

....

....

....

What passage of Scripture is one that a lot of people in your world are writing off as nonrelevant but that you find really makes an impact on your heart?

....

....

....

....

What is the most rebellious thing you did as a child?

....

....

....

....

....

....

....

....

"I still have streaks of rebellion in my heart, little punk rock stripes of green," says MK. What is the most rebellious thing in your life today?

....

....

....

....

....

....

....

....

PRAYER

God, I have times that I allow Your guardrails to become fodder for rebellion in my life. And I have times that I worship the "rules" and judge others by them more than I walk along Your guardrail of mercy. When I veer too far to one side or the other, help me move back to the crown of the road. Where there are guardrails in Your Word that I have ignored for too long, please let Your kind Counselor of the Holy Spirit whisper to my heart. Help me see the purpose behind Your guidance. Remind me that You love me enough to put bumpers on the corners and that You also love me enough to let me experience the consequences when I remove those bumpers. Thank You for Your forgiveness. In the name of Jesus, amen.

CHAPTER 15

LIFE ON THE HAMSTER WHEEL

Stuffing appeared to be the smartest hamster of the bunch. While his cage mates ran endlessly on a wheel to nowhere, Stuffing remained fat, happy, and chilling in the corner of the cage. It was love at first hamster sight for MK, and Stuffing was quickly adopted.

Stuffing's reticence to hit the circular cardio wasn't just a nod to his personality. He had a secret he was hiding beneath his fluff. Leave it to MK to come home with a hamster with three feet rather than four and to not realize it for a while. But the lesson Stuffing had to teach remained the same.

There's a lot to be said for not getting pulled into the spin cycle of busy.

You probably didn't think adulthood would be one big hamster wheel as a kid. From the outside looking in, #adulting looked more like getting to stay up as late as you wanted and being able to drive to the store and get cookies whenever the notion hit. And then the adult clock struck midnight, and you were in a loop you never anticipated, an alarm clock going off at obscene hours, a commute to the office that seemed never-ending, and a cycle of bills, interest, and debt that kept your bank account swirling the drain.

Ah, the joys of adulthood.

So many of us enter the vortex without realizing its gravitational pull. We're just trying to procure a place to live and some kind of vehicle to drive, after all. For MK, the early days of her marriage were marked by late shifts waitressing at the diner and a miraculous twenty-dollar bill showing up in the pages of her Bible, just in time for a date night with Ian. They used that date night to dream about how things would be when they had "real" jobs and careers and a "real" house bigger than their postage-stamp apartment, and there would be money for going to a "real" dinner rather than their date night Wendy's Frosty cuisine.

But almost a decade and a half later, things weren't quite what they had planned. Says MK,

Fourteen years into our relationship, we had claimed our American dream: a beautiful home, two golden retrievers, and cars that didn't rattle on the interstate. We had two healthy children and a circle of support to help raise them. After years of constant financial stress, it blew me away that we were having this conversation. In this moment, in New York City. With these stupid, overpriced salads. We had everything we'd ever wanted, and we were unhappy as we'd ever been.

As a result of that later date night, MK and Ian realized that they'd fallen into the trap of staying on the wheel, dizzy with achievement and procurement.

Entering the wheel and staying on the wheel can feel like you're being responsible. It can feel like going for your goals. It can feel like leadership and example-setting. It can feel like you're getting somewhere.

But it's important to look around while you run. Is your marriage better or worse? Is time with your family happier and more relaxing, or is it another nuisance? What about rest? Is that something you experience on a consistent basis, or is it something you think is for the weak? We build, strive, worry, run, circle, and achieve like it's all up to us. But Scripture reminds us:

Unless the LORD builds the house, the builders labor in vain. Unless the LORD watches over the city, the guards stand watch in vain. In vain you rise early and stay up late, toiling for food to eat—for he grants sleep to those he loves. (Psalm 127:1–2 NIV)

In our grit-and-grind culture today, we can lose sight of God working on our behalf. Yes, we have responsibilities to show up. We have responsibilities to honor our employers, be productive, and take care of our families. But the endless cycle of *more more more* keeps us running faster to hit a never-quite-reachable rung on the ladder. As King Solomon reminds us, "He who loves money will not be satisfied with money, nor he who loves abundance with its income" (Eccles. 5:10 NASB).

Have an honest conversation with yourself and if you're married, with your partner. What is enough? What if less really could be more? Are you happier now than you were before all the things needed to be purchased and decorated and updated and stored? As MK says, if you want peace, "you have to stay off the dang hamster wheel."

JOURNALING

What is an area of your life in which you suspect you might be running on a hamster wheel, an endless cycle of activity that doesn't seem to get you closer to God or peace? How did you get on that wheel?

....

....

....

Write about the messages surrounding achievement, prestige, and goals that you grew up with or took on as you entered adulthood. What wisdom do you find there? What toxicity might be there?

....

....

....

What is something today that brings you tremendous stress but you keep on doing? Why?

....

....

....

What are your fears about getting off the hamster wheel?

....

....

....

....

....

What is something you forecasted would be much better, would make you happier and more fulfilled, but upon arrival to that situation, you discovered it wasn't all you expected it to be?

....

....

....

....

....

....

In your today, what means more to you, peace or achievement? While they don't necessarily have to compete, they often do. Jot down some ideas for changes you can make to allow yourself to go for your goal while not outrunning peace and fulfillment in this moment, today, right now.

....

....

....

....

Take inventory:

What is bringing you fulfillment and joy today?

....

....

....

....

What isn't happy in your life today?

....

....

....

....

What are you willing to change to get off the hamster wheel?

....

....

....

....

PRAYER

God, I've allowed my goals, desires, and dreams to be shaped by the culture around me. I evaluate the purpose and success of my life by what others have and do and accomplish. Free me from this definition. Show me how to rewrite what fulfillment and happiness and joy mean. Forgive me for the times when You've provided and I've called it not enough. Forgive me for those times You've withheld something that would not have been good for me and I've thrown a fit. And give me the daring to determine what needs to stay in my life and what needs to go. Show me how to live in the most vibrant and peaceful way possible. In Jesus' name, amen.

CHAPTER 16

THE MESSINESS
WAS THE POINT

When it comes to nonfiction books, those that are in the self-help category are some of the most popular. From how to be more organized to tips on productivity, we gravitate toward things that we think will help us reduce the mess in our lives. And, sure, you'll find some helpful things in those books, and kudos to those authors.

But no matter how much we push back, file, and declutter, we can't outrun the debris field of twirling life. MK says, "I wish I could offer some revolutionary path that would allow you to sidestep your struggles. 'The Secret to a Mess-Free Life,' or something—a Bible study *with* a juice cleanse! I could write that book, and fill it with platitudes, and maybe Oprah would put it in her book club. But the reality is this: The world will continue to remain broken, and in it, we'll experience mess."

The flip side for some of us is that we think we're too big a mess for God ever to be able to use us. We've dived deep into thinking that our mess is a case that God can't crack, that all those other people out there who are doing great things and raising cute kids and making out with their husbands somehow have avoided having mess in their lives and ours trap us.

Neither of those perspectives, the idea that there should be no mess in the world and the idea that we're a bigger mess than anyone else, resides in truth. Jesus somehow combines both extremes and blends them into this powerful dichotomy: "I have told you these things, so that in me you may have peace. In this world you will have trouble. But take heart! I have overcome the world" (John 16:33 NIV).

MK reminds us, "Your rap sheet isn't impressive enough to break grace. There's no mind too dirty, no past too shady, that it can scare Jesus away. His death on the cross covered it all, so you could walk away clean." We might not realize our need for God if life wasn't a mess, *and* we'll miss the beauty if we see only the mess in life. It's a dance, one for which we have to practice the choreography every day.

There's no cure for being human. There *is* a cure for sin. There is healing from hurt, there is encouragement for today, there is learning from mistakes, and there is grace for blowing it. But God made us to be human. We are created in His image. He didn't make us from little beads of disinfected silicone.

He made us from the messy, life-giving, dusty dirt, that substance in which things grow and flourish. He sculpted us from the divine mess of His creation. Genesis 2:7 recounts, "Then the LORD God formed a man from the dust of the ground and breathed into his nostrils the breath of life, and the man became a living being" (NIV). Our origin story begins with the amniotic fluid of dust, and, one day, our physical bodies will become dust again, returning to a womb of soil.

MK says, "I am still a holy hot mess. I don't know if that's going to change. I still yell at my children; I still fight with my husband; I still eat packages of Oreos when I'm sad. In my heart I know that the things of this world will leave me wanting more."

It takes a big God to let His kids play in the mud puddles. It takes a big God to clean us up, even when we want to keep playing. Maybe that's the secret of being a holy hot mess when we realize that somehow, someway, God has space enough for the purifying process this life is taking us through while at the same time letting us make mud pies.

We are a mess. But we are God's mess. He is not surprised when we stomp through the church's front door with muddy feet. He's not taken aback when we forget to wash our hands before communing on the Eucharist of Christ. It doesn't throw Him when we peer into the windows of eternity and leave gritty fingerprints on the glass.

He knew it would happen. And He long ago established the remedy: "For I am convinced that neither death nor life, neither angels nor demons, neither the present nor the future, nor any powers, neither height nor depth, nor anything else in all creation, will be able to separate us from the love of God that is in Christ Jesus our Lord" (Rom. 8:38 NIV).

Not even our mess.

JOURNALING
· · · · · · · · · · · · · · · · ·

What habit have you long had that you don't like? What would happen if you accepted that habit as part of who you are?

....

....

Have you been in search of ultimate satisfaction on this earth? Do you think it's achievable?

....

....

What are some things today that you find you continue to search for? Do those things include purpose, connection, or love?

....

....

....

MK concludes the book by saying, "We are *holy* in our hot mess." Do you find that easy or difficult to receive? Why?

....

....

....

PRAYER
· · · · · · · · · · ·

Too often, God, I'm looking for ways to avoid the mess, temporariness, and uncertainty in this world. And so often, You use those very things to draw me closer to You, to remind me to rely on You, to trust You. Help me to see the mess as a reminder of Your holiness and provision. Help me to see the mess as evidence of my need for You. Help me to see the mess as the dusty workbench of the Messiah, where He makes all things new. And God, I ask that You make me holy in my mess until You call me home. In Jesus' name, amen.

SCRIPTURE CREDITS

Scripture quotations noted ESV are from the Holy Bible, English Standard Version. ESV® Text Edition: 2016. Copyright © 2001 by Crossway Bibles, a publishing ministry of Good News Publishers.

Scripture quotations noted GW are from the *God's Word*® translation. Copyright © 1995, 2003, 2013, 2014, 2019, 2020 by God's Word to the Nations Mission Society. All rights reserved.

Scripture quotations noted NASB are from the NEW AMERICAN STANDARD BIBLE. Copyright © 1960, 1962, 1963, 1968, 1971, 1972, 1973, 1975, 1977, 1995 by The Lockman Foundation. Used by permission. All rights reserved. http://www.lockman.org.

Scripture quotations noted NIV are taken from the Holy Bible, New International Version®. Copyright © 1973, 1978, 1984, 2011 by Biblica, Inc.™ Used by permission of Zondervan. All rights reserved worldwide. www.zondervan.com. The "NIV" and "New International Version" are trademarks registered in the United States Patent and Trademark Office by Biblica, Inc.™

ABOUT THE AUTHOR

Mary Katherine Backstrom is best known for her viral videos and candid writing on family, faith, and mental illness. She has been featured on *Today Show*, CNN, and *New York Times*—but her friends and family are most impressed with her one-time appearance on *Ellen*. MK resides in Alabama with her husband, children, two dogs, and a cat. When she isn't writing, MK is active in her church, her community, and her favorite Mexican restaurant.